# Confidential Reports

Immanuel Mifsud

*translated from the Maltese by*
Maurice Riordan

SOUTHWORD*editions*

First published in 2005
by Southword Editions,
the Munster Literature Centre,
Frank O'Connor House, 84 Douglas Street,
Cork, Ireland.

Set in Centaur
Printed in Ireland by Colour Books, Dublin.

ISBN: I-905002-08-4
www.munsterlit.ie

This book is the seventh in a series of thirteen published as
part of the official programme for Cork 2005: European
Capital of Culture

Cover Image: Pink Fall by Frieda Meaney Oil on Canvas,
2003

**Cork 2005**
European Capital of Culture

 PREMIER
PARTNER

Acknowledgements:

I am grateful to Adrian Grima for his assistance in translating this book.

Thanks are due to the editors of *Orient Express, Poetry London, Poetry Review, Southword, The Stinging Fly* and *Tall-Lighthouse*, where some of these translations have been published.

# Contents

# The Day of the Dead (in Bratislava)

If you were here, I'd ask you to recite
whole chapters that now are buried with dust.
Then I might have some clue as to how
I'd found my way to this unlit station.
From which no train is ever going to leave.
From which no footstep leads me away.

If you were here today, you could colour in
the blank map by which I was led alone
through the streets, the blind corners I turned
so that now I've arrived at this precise spot.
I've no idea how to pull myself out of here.

My blood, the fairground where ghouls hang out.

## Poem at Your Funeral

Ma, I remember you sitting out the back
peeling tangerines and telling me stories,
those tall stories you loved so much to spin.
Ma, I remember the day you told me
you saw the stars fall one by one from heaven,
so many the sea became a sea of lights.

Every night, lying awake, I remember you said
rain drops were Mary's darning needles,
and if I touched them they wouldn't prick;
that the wind was only the voice of God singing
and that the thunder and lightning-flashes
were playthings baby Jesus had let fall.

Ma, I remember you beautiful like red roses,
like jasmine, and narcissus, and marguerites.
Ma, I remember your voice quick as a fiddle
playing or falling silent as the fancy struck you.

Then it fell silent never to start again.
Even the flowers can hear the empty silence.
The sea lights have all been switched off.

Ma, it's time to go. Look, someone has lit the candles.
Someone is waiting to hand you a posy of flowers!
Be sure you smile.  Ma, happy Feast Day!

## Anniversary

You — the woman who loved me — are a year in the ground,
in the cold clay, in the dust, in the sand,
in the humid hole we dug for you to sleep in,
supposedly so we'd put to rest our memories.

You — the woman who loved me — are a year in the ground,
already one full year, and yet I can say
your voice comes back to me whenever
I listen to the flowers pray in the morning;
each time I stifle a cry, as you showed me to do,
so one dies at a steady pace, without too many jolts;
each time I give a rose, so I too get chucked away.

You — the woman who loved me — are a year in the ground,
and I can say, as I piece together your face
from the yellowing linen canvas of the past,
only you knew the heaviness of being a poet,
spilling his offspring with each step he takes.
Only you knew the weight on the burdened feet
of your son, counting the dry hours frittered away
with each sun that lets itself go on the vast waters
which I wish I could grasp the edges of.

## Some Leaves from Paris

I wanted to meet you here –
by the window with the sun
going down outside, while the room lounges
to the sounds of Jacques Brel
whose songs amplify the darkness
which is about to overwhelm
the silence of Versailles
as one more day adds itself to the rest.

I wanted to meet you here –
by this bunch of white roses
already on the wane
beside the piano set up for romance
near the image that has slipped from my face
near Mme. Emptiness my companion.

I wanted to meet you here –
so you'd see I'm an outcast and a drifter
one with no great expectations
one readily lost among the hordes
striding with maps in their hands
one attentive to the voices of all who address me
one still living the old fairy tale.

I wanted to meet you here.
But you had mislaid the ticket to the terminus
and I'd forgotten what your face was like.

# This Dark-Eyed Man

He walks slowly this dark-eyed man,
he feels the cold despite the blazing sun.
His blood is full of burning chemicals,
his veins are ice-cold and about to rupture.

He walks slowly always alone.
He knows how to cast a single look of dejection.
He never could sing and has forgotten how to talk.
His name is lost because he gave it to someone
who had no ears or face to see and hear him.

Today he visited the clinic
and spread the colour of his eyes around the cold room.
Again he tried to remember his name,
maybe here he'll find someone to listen and see,
maybe he can hand in his red poem,
the one so shamelessly stuck in a vein,
maybe he can take off the thick jacket
he once used as a blanket for his body.

Today he visited a clinic and once again
he found a yellowing prescription there for him.

# Confidential Reports – in the Form of a
## Public-Private Confession

He says he used to watch the Devil masturbate.
He says he'd tell him while he was praying
to go down and lick the evil off the world.
He says he enjoyed it.  He started to have faith.
He would cut himself to see the black blood
sprinkle its mysterious blessing on the night.
And at the full moon he'd shout out the Mass
up in the hills where no-one could hear it.
He'd fallen for a woman who'd choked to death,
who smiled at him from a grave, left slightly ajar.
That way, she could see the moon swell up in the evenings.
He says he tried to give her the son she craved.
He tried twice but he failed on both occasions.

He used to worship the dark. Then the dark abducted him.

*

Her brother was putting her to sleep.
And he touched her swelling body
where the rust-brown blood seeped out.
They heard their father pant in the night,
their mother hushing him with her hand.
For even the sins of marriage must be hidden.
She was aroused by her brother's fingers,
by her father's noise, her mother's raw silence.
It was as if it rained inside her body, or the ice
turned to water and mixed with the water
of her brother moving on top of her.

Then out of the blue a boy was born
with a moon-face and a voice that frightened her.
He cried for six days before he stopped.
They buried him in the corner of a field.

She loved in the dark. And the dark loved her mind.

*

She vowed in front of her three children
she would never again sleep beside her husband –
not after the filthy beds of the men
he went to every day behind her back.
She'd found him out in broad daylight,
her husband, the father of her children.

*

That quiet bisexual man
is always hovering near the front door,
leaning out when the sun comes up,
in the hope she'll give him a face to look at,
in the hope he might know at last the shape
his own dark look should take.
Every night he says he dreams his face has died
and in the dream it becomes a belladonna lily.
His nails grow sharp and turn bright red,
the colour of his handsome rosebud mouth.
He's out on the open sea, his broad hips
stirring the waves, his chest full with milk.

In the morning he finds he hasn't shaved that week.

## Weariness

We stroll together barefoot, until we reach
the shore, our hands listless at our sides.
Weariness is the old woman beckoning us
to stop walking on this winding road,
to let ourselves free-fall into the sea,
to let the waves show us the road as before.

There is nothing to do but sit at anchor;
the white lassitude hangs from our mouths;
some sand takes soundings from its slumber,
some lukewarm spindrift falls with a splash;
a slight squall, looking for a place to curl up;
an old moon, shedding tears in his sleep.

# I'd Dreamt This Dream Already

Look: even my solitude has died.
Every time I walk I see many walking
behind, in front, beside me walking
with their hands, their eyes, locked in mine; walking
near me, at rest or upright. Always walking.
They even drink the tears I weep.
Stride after stride, while my face disintegrates
and they pick its remains from the ground.
Stride after stride, while I clear the way ahead.
Stride after stride, and they are always walking:
behind, in front, beside me; walking
near me, resting or upright. Always walking.
I can feel the warmth from their looks.
I even feel the rain that washes them.
I even feel their legs strain to give birth
to more faces to look at me, looking.

Stride after stride, I've dreamt this dream already
when emerging old from the vagina
to find innumerable hands of welcome.
That day also, I'd already dreamt this dream.

## Poem in Front of a Slightly Scratched Mirror

Bear in mind you're just a minor story,
missing both its first and final parts.

Bear in mind you're just the doubtful echo
that broke a two hundred years' lull in halves.

# The Mad People

In the electronic age every nutcase
with a laptop is writing a masterpiece.
They spend their nights locked up in chat rooms
and emerge with red eyes and love poems.

# Le Grand Tango

*homage to Astor Piazzolla*

I

With darkness in your eyes, out you go and dance the
                                                    tango.
A voice is shouting in your ribcage: watch out,
Your blood will splatter your white countenance!
Quick, press me to you, I'll smear you with my blood.
Me, I'm nothing, a hot body and a tall story.

In the darkness of your eyes, out I go and dance the tango.

I'm all your poems in one slim volume.
I'm the adolescent boy about to strip
in the open-air gardens of the city.
I'm the remains of cellular messages
I'm the blood-drop sick at heart.
Slowly, this last tango will escort you
lingering as it makes it bow and leaves.
Who you are or where you're from
I do not ask but press you to me.

You who're nothing, a hot body and a tall story.

2

Our delinquency has travelled far and wide
in foreign streets in the small hours of nights.

We've visited rooms far off and others close at hand,
we visited bodies we've scarcely known,
we bedded down as guests at strange addresses.

We've sought the death-wish in the embrace
and found it in our breathless pleasures.

## 3

How sad the tango sounds tonight –
as if darkened by the scudding clouds;
as if gravid now with tears; and broken,
having mislaid the harmonies
it drew from your body and mine, when we were tangled in
the threadbare sheets of mystery.

How empty are the gazes we pin
upon our faces, now the dark
prepares the funeral of our days.

Tonight the tango is so sad for me –
sad like a waterless stretch of sand,
sad like an exquisite tawny flower bent in pain,
sad like mile on mile of empty autobahn,
sad like the black pupils peering through the tears,
sad like the exhalation of this poem.

## Now You Sleep

Now you sleep – I can smell your dead hand
in the small of my back, in its pool of sweat,
and my conscience, that familiar old piss-head,
staggers between the now and the not-yet.

When you wake – dishevelled, demure –
the sun will highlight that ugly look
lost among the sheets full of shy stories,
stories we lugged up from the basement,
stories we hid under the pillows of flowers,
flowers that will certainly wither by noon.

## The One Hundred and One Lovers

Now that I've taken that same road
taken by the hundred lovers before me,
instruct me in the movements of the tango
we danced yesterday by the open window,
when the sly breeze crept in without a sound,
dragging with it a smell of indigo – not unlike
the outlandish stories I gave birth to.

Now I've managed to see you in the night
which falls when you take off your clothes,
instruct me well in the steps of this tango
and in the off-key music coming out of me
and in the warm water that comes out of you.

# Poem for Nina

Once I saw you dissolve into the sky's blue,
and into the blue of the sea water.
Once I saw you wear a blue straw hat
and I wanted to die, and to live forever.

Once I dreamed the sea stole the colour from your face,
and the tips of the waves took your eyes' hue,
and I said: *let her gather her hair as a fountain,*
*let her gaze swim in the despondency of my eyes.*

Look, how the rain falls, and in the background falls
a singing troupe of souterrain women
who will rise again on a moonless night.

Look, how the rain falls, and with it falls
your portrait, the one of old, painted
with dull colours trickling on the glass.

## The Clock

*a version*

You know no-one can deny the clock.
Every time I look at you I see
an old hurt that's always growing,
spreading with the wrinkles on your face.

There's an end walking in step with every beginning.
There's an edge towards which we're moving without
                                            wanting it.
There are different streets for us two.

## Dust and Sand

You came into my room like its film of dust,
like the streetwise sand stuck between my toes,
with the smell of limestone on your breath
and the fine grit polishing your eyes.

## The Rough Water in your Dark Eyes

I realized from the rough water in your dark eyes,
from your hesitation in the presence of flowers,
from the crash of the sea whispering in your mouth…

that you are one more sweet child of the wind.

# Once Again You Remind Me Without Knowing

Once again you remind me without knowing:
of the large and empty spaces that killed me,
of the depths of the sea that left me breathless,
of the smoke-filled clouds that swore to finish me off,
of the face of a woman tall with the verdict of guilt.

Don't squash me again because next time
I'm leaving in the caravan I've kept waiting,
in a ship that disappears over the horizon,
on a one-way express train into the night,
on a flight that gets me out of here for good.

# The Five Wounds of the Night Sand

### 1.

What's the use of you laying me down at night
if I'm perished beside you, if I lose my way
in the dark light you give off, if the silence
from your cold mouth makes me go deaf?
I've started to tremble looking at your white face,
and I've no memory of what your lips are like.

### 2.

Don't you worry... there are no beautiful flowers left:
I gave them all to you and now I've found them
on the floor, buried under a story of sand,
under the miles of memory-erasing dust.
Under a pile of words I've found the flowers
that bled to death, the flowers without colours.

### 3.

Your breath comes like the waves always breaking,
like great sea horses stretching themselves out on the strand.

### 4.

There's a tear emerging from this sand castle
exactly from the spot where I once stuck a most beautiful
                                                    rose
and the waves pulled it off intent on killing it.

### 5.

Let me die in silence. Go. Don't stay.
Let me become white as your wordless face.
Let me depart quietly from this place.

## And Then You Sleep

And then you sleep. And forget. Forget
the long trek it took to reach me here,
forget the dark and heavy nights of heartache,
forget the river of tears that ran between us,
forget the avowal of love, so weary now
it's needs to sit down and have a little rest,
forget the bad dream that keeps reminding you.

Then you turn and you sleep. And forget.
You give me the worn out gaze of an invalid
and leave me to welcome a new sun alone.
You leave me to look at you and start to cry.
You leave me to lie on the sand on my own
and I die a final death before I'm murdered
in front of this shifting sea of worthless silver.
You leave me wither. You leave me finish.
You leave me end. Leave me buried under rubble.

## The Taste of Blood

Look: this blood has the taste of flowers,
you don't know if it's my blood or
the juice of roses or white jasmine.
But your mouth is full of burning sand.

Now what will happen if by the time you spit the sand out
I've lost all my blood down to the last drop?

## Your Hands Are Always Searching

They walk. Your hands always walk. They search
for the little boy running about with one hand
in the sea, the other high in the air.
They walk. Your hands always walk. They search
for the boy whose eyes popped out and landed
in the flowers, flowers that wake up wet
shedding their cold tears in all weathers.

And your hands walking follow him closely.

No, I can see it won't take long to find him,
since he's still running around without his eyes.
They're walking, they're looking for those hands,
so that they can kill him at the first touch.

## In Silence the Leaves Are Falling

I knew by now the story must repeat itself,
that in the middle of the night you were going to scream,
leaving me half dead on the mattress
where the beautiful ghosts had once come
and you lay them down for a night at your side.

There's a book in which they printed all the stories
and when I open it sometimes to read,
stale tears gather in the shape of a tree
with a very long trunk that seems to touch the sky
with all its leaves falling in silence to the ground.

## Trees

It's said the trees round here sometimes walk,
that they follow a path down to the river.
They spend the day looking at the water.
They walk back up again when it's dark.

## Poems in the Rain

The rain is like your hands on my back.
Some drops trickle, others stick on the thin glass,
my only shelter from the world.
The rain falls, tap-tapping the glass
to remind me that every moment
may be the last.  And that will be it,
because the sun will have set,
erasing us much like a layer of dust.

*

I look and I find you sleeping
even though my hands are still in yours.
My arms are tired of pulling at you.
You're one more wall I'm tired of having to climb.
I hear the rain and start to cry.

*

I had thought my garden was starting to smell nicely,
that it opened a road where I could walk
and it would lead one day to the sea.

I had thought my flowers had a scent
which would comfort the weak and bring them rest,
it would help them in their grief and give them health.

Instead I heard the breath suffer another defeat,
I heard the uproar and havoc as the rain
pounded the soft trunks, the petals, the beautiful smell.
And I find myself alone once again.

35

I lie in the mud letting the rain wash me.
It falls on my face, it hugs me, it makes me cry,
It shows me the river bank, so I might fall in
and drown, struggling for air.  And find rest thereby.

✳

Shall we undress?  I'll show you my wounds,
how they run all around my body
like rivers of poisonous blood,
how it turns to water, tears, salty rain.

Shall I give you the whole story,
how I'm being frog-marched along this precipice?
You want to know me? Would you like a clue to my name?
Shall I let you hold my face to your breasts?

*Stay away, I love you more from afar.*
*Your wounds can't compare to mine.*
*Stay away, I hurt you less from afar.*
*Look at me, I bleed as well as you.*

*I've a long sad story to relate.*
*No flower can cure its smell,*
*no poem, no-one's smiling face,*
*no-one's colour — yours least of all.*

I/you wanted to give birth to a green tree.
But you don't recognize the strange fruit of my face.
I/you wanted to give birth to a great tree.
But you don't recognize the warm tears of my poem.

Look, maybe you'll see the rain that's falling;
look and you'll see its black embrace;
you'll see how much these flowers put up with
every time they feel neglected;
look closely, maybe you'll catch a glimpse of me
at the front door to the beautiful house,
boarded up, so I'll not catch sight of you.

## Last Night

I will kneel to flick away the yellow sand.
Between your toes I find red flowers.
They have a strong smell of last night,
of the long night we spent loving the sea,
of the night we spent listening to the wind.

You sang. You could hardly be heard.
You sang. Your eyes were closed,
looking at me while I was closing my eyes
so I could hear that love of the sea,
hear the hammer-beat of your chest wall,
the blood struggling in your arteries,
hear the baby crying in your womb,
hear the windows creak open for me,
so I might go inside, so I might be close to you.

I'll impregnate your thighs while they're still wet,
splashed by the mischievous spindrift.
And I'll watch your eyes close once more
for the long night we spent loving the copper moon
that sprouted from a black sea.
Between your toes I find red flowers.
They have a distinct smell of last night,
the same smell as your night-coloured hair.
I understood the night had the same taste as you,
the taste of the wind and the taste
of the sea, and the taste of the moon,
the taste of the flowers, the same taste
of the dew trickling down your open thighs.
While we were loving the sea you started to sing.
Your eyes were closed and you could hardly be heard.
You were welcoming the night inside you. You were

sending infra-red waves from your warm blood.
You were giving birth. You were dying by degrees.

I wake up, and I find the wind is from the North-East.

## Tango Lujurioso

Like sand trickled between the fingers
this tango comes from the flute of my love.
*Ti-tum ti-tum* it goes, then gathers tempo
until it's in step with the flexing motion
of your body. A morning will break
when you will miss the presence of the sun, or
we'll wake together sunburnt on a blue strand,
tired and weak, with the smell troubling you
of a summer no longer ours. A morning will break
when the flute is silent, or it plays a little.
Or we may die as soon as the tango is over.
Or we may forget that once, like the sand
between your fingers, we broadcast this love.

Now my sorrow will dance with your body,
angular, sand-stained, and darkly shadowed
where the blue moonlight slips between us –
the beautiful girl who asked never to be born.
Now my sorrow will dance, with the peach tree
that surveys me from the blue distance.
Your eyes are slightly apart like your lips
in prayer for more, always more, more, more...
How alone is this lassitude of the body –
how long this strand of hair in my mouth...
It comes like some river of dew from the core
of a rose to wet me, comes to wash me,
comes to take me by the hand and lift me up
so that I may rise and enter sweetly,
moving in time with the tango that longs to prance
in the enclosure of this lassitude beneath me,
open, waiting for the moment to break.

Now get up, let's climb down to the hidden water,
let us rinse the red fire from our cheeks in plenty of water.
Up you get, let's go down into the cold water –
feel yourself relax on its languid mattress,
feel the lilies on the surface float to your side,
feel the cold licking at your feverish body,
feel the choppy water rinse you out.
Let's go down and peer into the white night,
into its deepest pool.

## Still Life

There's this candle floating in water.
It breaks into song, a *milonga* that reminds me
of my own story drifting towards a hidden edge.
Afterwards, I hear its faint echo,
then nothing – a story that never occurred.

*

There's a white flame half-way to my eyes,
as and I shed tears to the tune of a slick tango.
The dead soul of a woman who means to take
my heart and kill it is half-way up my chest.
Around me a blood-red fire flares into life.

*

There's this photo left on the table
of a woman stroking her hair at the seaside.
This woman looks at me and invites me
to stroke my hair too, so I do my best
to lie flat on the table and become a photo.

*

The books are left in the candle-light.
In the flames dance the silent poems
of two old poets delivering the lines
of two young poets who've just learned about the sea,
of two poets all set to eat each other.

*

Two glasses overflowing with pear nectar,
two plates with chicken and raw vegetables,
an ashtray also, stuffed with cigarette butts,
beside a bowl of stories from the past,
and in the background the tango going berserk.

42

*

On this red napkin are written down
a few scraps of my  disorderly life.
The perfumed notes of the *bandoneón* produce
broad fields and valleys of bubbling blood –
I have a wash, so I'll smell nice in the morning.


*

When the night's gone and the candles are snuffed,
when the tango stops and everything's unplugged,
when I start my car and drive off
along empty roads full of sad people,
you will kiss the darkness and the silence again.

## The Tenth of September

Don't let the wind remind you anymore of me,
because it's up to no good letting us
think we're gathering flowers — but when
we get a proper look at them we'll see
every single one was nipped in the bud.

The wind likes to play games. It likes to have a good laugh
at people like us who are caught in its arms.

## The Thirteenth of September

Today I won't even sleep: I'll hang about and watch
while you run around, disappearing like the shoreline.
In the morning, when you wake up, you'll find
I'm still watching, my eyes the same colour as the sea floor,
the sea that brought you to me, much to my surprise.

# The Nineteenth of September

It's a ship leaving harbour right this minute,
sitting pretty on the waves – while the land pulls away,
taking with it old memories,
short stories full of heart break.

It's the last note of a score
played by the flute when it sucked the breath from my body
taking with it everything inside me.

It's the first rain of September
sucked in by the parched earth of August.

This minute is the last minute and we're on board.

# The Twentieth of September

They stream out of the accordion like youngsters
with long curly hair down to their ankles.
And they go out into the wind on the open sea
and count the waves coming to rest at their feet.

They stream out of the accordion like pensioners,
their eyes dejected and bleary-red.
They walk and walk on the road to tomorrow.

They stream out like nameless notes.
And I'm like the one you can barely hear.

Like a note that has no wish to end.

## A Message from October

Rest now, m'dear, you've come to the end of the road.
You're tired and the soles of your feet have worn out.
See, you're leaving a bright red trail behind you.
Besides your eyes are weak and you're going bald.
M'dear, it's time you were weaned from the breast.

What's this affliction that makes you still hang on in there?

What makes you chase the night in the belief you'll
                                        understand it?
What prompts you to get up and have another go,
when you know that nothing, not a single thing, is true?
Why can't you believe what the old girl said,
her great big eyes looking into yours.
There's no hope for you: you were born with the mark,
with the red cross right next to your name.
How can you still dream about erasing it all?
Why do you want to swim against a river in flood?
Look at you spit blood from your bruised mouth.
Look at you trying to shout when your voice is gone.
Look at you wanting to get up and walk on those dislocated
                                        legs,
your only support the stems of bored-looking flowers,
flowers that have grown tall and weak and spindly.
Look at you writing out the long list of the tragedies,
and you persist in forcing one more story with the rest.

Stop, you dimwit, stop this minute. It's not true
there's a blue sea waiting to take you in its arms.
Stop dreaming it will rise from behind the mountains.
Behind the hills are only more big ugly hills.

## Tonight Dress Me in your Mourning-Coloured Hair

Tonight dress me in your mourning-coloured hair,
wrap me up in its satin pleats and folds.
Come, dress me in your dripping wet hair,
come and dress me in hair dripping with sweat.

Let me read these pages you've written
between your legs, gripping me with the strength
of a carpenter's vice.  So I'll never get out.
There's a whole bible written in there, written
with blood, with tears of love, with sweat —
with your sweat, my sweat — with semen.
I have appended my own chapter to the bible.
That way, I can read the poems it contains,
chew over their images, taste them in my mouth.

Tonight dress me in your mourning-coloured hair.

## Her Body Wakes Up in the Shape of a Poem

Her body wakes up in the shape of a poem
stirring in the night for some love.
Her body woke up, turned to me so I could hear:
*I want the salt-sea in my mouth;*
*I want the sea in my every pore —*
*I want it, want it for me alone.*

I climb her face, my black clouds full of rain.
I climb to decorate her lips as they part.
I hear her get wet, as I cloud her over
and drip drop onto her a rough sea
for her to swim, be lost, and drown in.

> Take me: I'm the sea that wants to master you.
> I'm the thunder cloud pregnant with rain.
> I'm this moment you want never to be over.
> I'm the silent pause before the stifled shout
> of the woman who's taken the sea in her mouth.

We've pieced together a long poem
which shouldl still be wet in the morning.
Don't hang it up. Or put it outside to dry.
Then if you're thirsty you can have a drink.
And when I'm thirsty I'll find you there, damp.

# Her Long Legs White as Paper

Here's this ballerina pirouetting on the tips
of her long legs as white as paper,
the waist slender, arms shaping the air,
hair drawn tight in a bun, her expression hidden.

And sometimes the wind calls on me.
But the ballerina continues to pirouette,
not wanting me to wake up and see who's knocking.
She only wants me to watch while her body
turns into an old dream from my childhood,
turns into white paper on which I can write down
the important dates that have passed in my life.
A sad smile that is smeared with blood.

The red colour on her lips is like blood,
this ballerina pirouetting on the tips
of her long legs as white as paper,
as white as her expressionless eyes,
and as white as the music to which
the ballerina pirouettes on this box
that plays whenever decide to wind it.

## You Are My New Religion

You are my new religion,
a god in the form of a beautiful woman.

Ready to nail yourself to the cross on my chest:
waiting at my thigh for the scourge.

# Madrigal

### 1

A woman is naked at the edge of the rocks waving
to the emptiness that was inside her a moment ago.

### 2

*Come inside me, shower of cold rain.*
*Wash me well inside. Arouse me*
*for this eager moon that's waiting here.*
*I am that woman who walks in the rain.*
*I am that flower coiling with the water.*

### 3

Now that the rain has stopped I can hear your breath
sing hush-a-bye to send me to sleep.
But I still have this ardour to love you,
to wander about in the dark interior.

### 4

Her body is the colour of the orchestra of depressives;
her voice too reflects their colouring;
the same goes for her lassitude on the bed.

Only her expression has been painted without colour.

### 5

The voice of a blue lady who is barely heard.

Far-off: the voice of pleasure and of water,
the voice of dreaming and of weeping, the voice
of summer lightning, a voice of lightning, hers.

## 6

The smell of milk stirred with honey.
Your smell that makes me want to touch you,
I swim to you through the lukewarm water.

## 7

Vanilla from your breasts beckons to me.
The water turbid with soap smells of honey.
Pause. The sound of your body slipping into the water.

# Some Leaves from Mallorca

## Verses from Formentor Bay

### I

As soon as she saw the water she pulled up her skirt
and ran in up to her waist, an invitation to the waves.
And her fingers went tentacling across the bottom
looking for where she'd put her foot next in the sea,
which to my mind was her expectant lover.

> *I found the sea waiting for me. He gave me a smile.*
> *I found him fresh and eager for me.*
> *I undressed so he could see what I look like.*
> *He asked me to bend down, quickly, and do it.*
> *He asked me inside him and he'd go inside me.*
> *He asked me to keep on singing until I came.*

Then I left my song drifting on the white foam.

### 2

A Catalan poet lying on the sand
opened his arms to welcome the sea into him.
He spoke using the waves, then sang using the sand.
He wanted to say: *this is the Mediterranean*
*out of which these mountains rose into the sky.*
*This is the sea that swims in poetry.*
*This is the sea that runs with blue ink,*
*scribbling long cryptic poems on the rocks*
*which only the sea itself pauses to unravel.*

## 3

The sea is a muscular and virile man,
waiting for the first woman to come his way.
The sea is a beautiful, small-boned woman
waiting for her first man to come along,
so he'll turn into a poem full of blood
spreading out on the white linen.

## 4

The sea makes its approach slowly. Calmly.
With the soft-spoken ways of the sad. Sadly.
With the manner of someone old and patient.
It comes towards you to wet you, to love you,
to make you dance, to lay you down in sleep.

The sea makes its approach slowly. Calmly.

## 5

You play with water like a little girl.
You roll up your jeans and tie back your hair,
and you laugh when you skim the pebble
on the flat surface of the sea in Formentor.

Your eyes are the colour that comes upon me
when I remember this is just one more journey
along with all the others I'm collecting.
And I recall you're another story without an end.

# Some Leaves from Lahti and Helsinki

While you're looking out the window
of this quiet three-star hotel,
your eyes are at some distant point you alone can see,
you and the mob of seagulls screaming
in the midnight sun, on a day that's broken loose
when your back is naked, your face averted,
your hands raised against the glass,
the curtains open, the sun streaming in
to sit on the bed as if it has some hunch
our first night is about to come to pass.

While you're looking out the window
you talk to the gulls in a voice that's violet-blue –
where we met beside the lake you smiled
as you said you spent your whole life crying:
like the screaming gulls, like the chords of the blues.
Your back is naked, your face averted,
and perhaps there's a tear sliding down
over your lips as they start to tremble.
And perhaps, but I can only guess, there's a look of age
I haven't seen before. Since it's just appeared.

In this room of a three-star hotel,
I called you and you came... or so I think...
Your naked back looks at me. You
look outside at a sun going down
that won't go down but keeps its eye on us.
It even comes inside to lie on the bed
as we get together, as we start to tangle,
as we start to undo the distance between us.
And you tell me without looking round
the old legend of the white rose
that becomes, as soon as it gets dark,

a hungry black tiger roaming
every nook and cranny for its prey;
round and round it goes before it closes in,
and right here, in the hotel room,
this very tiger starts tearing me apart
in time to the screaming of the gulls.

Between your cries, you make the big confession:
*My love, I wish I'd held onto my virginity!*
*Then I'd have wet you with my maiden blood.*
Stay still, let me search among the blues
and violets whether I can find my daughter
hiding somewhere under a shawl of black cloth,
under the shadow cast by these flexing muscles,
here, in this three-star hotel room
where I see a woman with the face of a girl
cry with pleasure, pleasure without blood-letting.
The sun too sees a woman with the face of a girl.
Even the gull wants to come in and hug her.

You said: *I choke on the sorrow.* You position me
under you to show the scratches on your chest;
to show me your breath going out and in –
going out towards the sun that won't go down,
going in to meet me in there –
inside you, while you continue to let go of tears
that start to light up in the midnight sun.

# Some Leaves from Brno

*On the Terrace of Dům Pánů z Lipé*

Take a photo so you'll always remember me.
Tomorrow we'll go back where we came from:
you to vanish among those fearful mountains,
me to drown at the bottom of the blue sea.

Take a photo of me on this roof of sadness.
In my eyes there are rivers of tears
eager to run in the hope of cooling off
just as the wet ink of this poem has gone cold.

Take a photo so you'll always remember me.
Tomorrow you'll forget: tomorrow will soon be here.

## In Udolni Street

This sadness is like those mountains of yours
which lord it over me on every tram we board.
It's like the empty streets of Brno.

It's like the silence fast asleep on Udolni Street.
It's like the circuitous journey we've made alone
since that day we met in the square.
It's like these soul-free pavements.

## The Rose of Gold

I put a rose of gold around your finger.
Gold never withers they say.
                              Tell me, is it true?

# One Night I Dreamt of the Old Gypsy

You have to keep on, despite the exhaustion.
Despite the need for sleep keep your eyes open.
I did warn you, son, you were born on the wrong day.
As to what's got you into this fix, never mind.
I told you, life's a freak show from start to finish.
I even told you not one flower would hold out.
But you have to keep going. Somebody has to man
the oars. And let whatever turns up turn up.

## Do You Remember?

Do you remember the man you climbed naked
with white hot skin, your eyes searching
for the soul long since drowned
in the seas he'd crossed to find you?

Remember him laughing by the river?
At the gulls overhead, at the tourists
coming and going on the streets?

This morning I saw him crushed under a leaf
which had fallen before its time.

# A Question

Look at me, pretty lady: is it true
that whoever crosses the ocean
and comes to this sad land of yours
ends up bloodless, with broken bones?